WENDY WATSON'S

Frog Went A-Courting

WENDY WATSON'S

Frog Went A-Courting

LOTHROP, LEE & SHEPARD BOOKS

NEW YORK

For Lewis,
always

First Edition 1 2 3 4 5 6 7 8 9 10

Library of Congress Cataloging in Publication Data
Watson, Wendy. Wendy Watson's Frog went a-courting / by Wendy Watson.
p. cm. Summary: Presents the well-known folk song about the courtship and marriage of the frog and the mouse. Includes music. ISBN 0-688-06539-2. —ISBN 0-688-06540-6 (lib. bdg.) 1. Folk songs. [1. Folk songs.] I. Frog he would a-wooing go (Folk song) II. Title. III. Title: Frog went a-courting. PZ8.3.W345Fr 1990 782.42162'0268—dc20
89-63022 CIP AC

Frog went a-courting and he did ride,
   Um-hmm,
Frog went a-courting and he did ride,
   Um-hmm.
Frog went a-courting and he did ride
With a sword and pistol by his side,
   Um-hmm, um-hmm, um-hmm.

He rode up to Miss Mouse's hall,
 Um-hmm,
He rode up to Miss Mouse's hall,
 Um-hmm.
He rode up to Miss Mouse's hall,
Loud and lovely he did call,
 Um-hmm, um-hmm, um-hmm.

He said, Miss Mouse, are you within?
   Um-hmm,
He said, Miss Mouse, are you within?
   Um-hmm.
He said, Miss Mouse, are you within?
Yes, kind sir, I sit and spin!
   Um-hmm, um-hmm, um-hmm.

He took Miss Mouse upon his knee,
    Um-hmm,
He took Miss Mouse upon his knee,
    Um-hmm.
He took Miss Mouse upon his knee,
And he said, Miss Mouse, will you marry me?
    Um-hmm, um-hmm, um-hmm.

Oh no, kind sir, I can't do that,
  Um-hmm,
Oh no, kind sir, I can't do that,
  Um-hmm.
Oh no, kind sir, I can't do that
Without consent of Uncle Rat,
  Um-hmm, um-hmm, um-hmm.

Old Uncle Rat he soon came home,
    Um-hmm,
Old Uncle Rat he soon came home,
    Um-hmm.
Old Uncle Rat he soon came home,
Says, Who's been here since I've been gone?
    Um-hmm, um-hmm, um-hmm.

There's been a pretty young gentleman,
    Um-hmm,
There's been a pretty young gentleman,
    Um-hmm.
There's been a pretty young gentleman
Who says he'll marry me if he can,
    Um-hmm, um-hmm, um-hmm.

Uncle Rat laughed and shook his sides,
   Um-hmm,
Uncle Rat laughed and shook his sides,
   Um-hmm.
Uncle Rat laughed and shook his sides
To think his niece would be a bride,
   Um-hmm, um-hmm, um-hmm.

Then Uncle Rat he went to town,
  Um-hmm,
Then Uncle Rat he went to town,
  Um-hmm.
Then Uncle Rat he went to town
To buy Miss Mouse a wedding gown,
  Um-hmm, um-hmm, um-hmm.

Where shall the wedding supper be?
   Um-hmm,
Where shall the wedding supper be?
   Um-hmm.
Where shall the wedding supper be?
Way down yonder in the hollow tree,
   Um-hmm, um-hmm, um-hmm.

What shall the wedding supper be?
    Um-hmm,
What shall the wedding supper be?
    Um-hmm.
What shall the wedding supper be?
Three green beans and a black-eyed pea,
    Um-hmm, um-hmm, um-hmm.

First to come in was Bumblebee,
    Um-hmm,
First to come in was Bumblebee,
    Um-hmm.
First to come in was Bumblebee
With his fiddle on his knee,
    Um-hmm, um-hmm, um-hmm.

The next to come in was Missus Snake,
   Um-hmm,
The next to come in was Missus Snake,
   Um-hmm.
The next to come in was Missus Snake,
Bringing around the wedding cake,
   Um-hmm, um-hmm, um-hmm.

And then here came old Reverend Bug,
    Um-hmm,
And then here came old Reverend Bug,
    Um-hmm.
And then here came old Reverend Bug,
He took his seat by the cider jug,
    Um-hmm, um-hmm, um-hmm.

Next to come in was a little seed-tick,
    Um-hmm,
Next to come in was a little seed-tick,
    Um-hmm.
Next to come in was a little seed-tick,
He ate so much it made him sick,
    Um-hmm, um-hmm, um-hmm.

Then they sent for Doctor Fly,
    Um-hmm,
Then they sent for Doctor Fly,
    Um-hmm.

Then they sent for Doctor Fly,
He said, Young fellow, you almost died,
    Um-hmm, um-hmm,
    Um-hmm.

Late to come was a nimble flea,
   Um-hmm,
Late to come was a nimble flea,
   Um-hmm.
Late to come was a nimble flea,
He danced a jig for the bumblebee,
   Um-hmm, um-hmm, um-hmm.

But then crept in an old bobcat,
   Um-hmm,
But then crept in an old bobcat,
   Um-hmm.
But then crept in an old bobcat,
And he put a stop to all of that!
   Um-hmm, um-hmm, um-hmm.

So that was the end of the wedding day,
  Um-hmm,
So that was the end of the wedding day,
  Um-hmm.
So that was the end of the wedding day,
And now I have no more to say,
  Um-hmm, um-hmm, um-hmm.

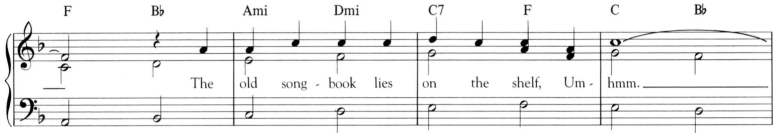
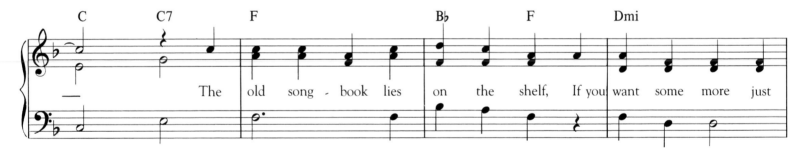
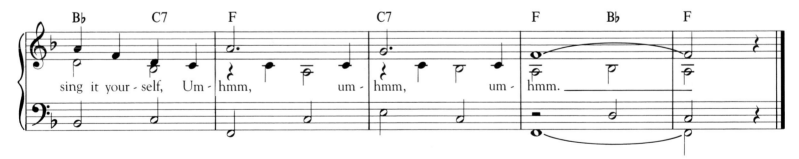

Piano arrangement by Paul Alan Levi